THE WORLD'S WORST NATURAL DISASTERS

THE WORLD'S WORST
HURRICANES

by John R. Baker

raintree

a Capstone company — publishers for children

Raintree is an imprint of Capstone Global Library Limited, a company incorporated in England and Wales having its registered office at 264 Banbury Road, Oxford, OX2 7DY – Registered company number: 6695582

www.raintree.co.uk
myorders@raintree.co.uk

Edited by Aaron Sautter
Designed by Steve Mead
Picture research by Jo Miller
Production by Tori Abraham
Originated by Capstone Global Library Limited
Printed and bound in China

ISBN 978 1 474 72479 1 (hardback)
20 19 18 17 16
10 9 8 7 6 5 4 3 2 1

ISBN 978 1 474 72483 8 (paperback)
21 20 19 18 17
10 9 8 7 6 5 4 3 2 1

British Library Cataloguing in Publication Data
A full catalogue record for this book is available from the British Library.

Acknowledgements
We would like to thank the following for permission to reproduce photographs:
Alamy: Chronicle, 10–11; AP Images: Harry Koundakjian, 12–13; Getty Images: The LIFE Picture Collection/Peter Stackpole, 22–23; NASA: Earth Observatory, 26–27; Newscom: EPA/Vincent Laforet, 16–17, Mirrorpix/Slater Arnold, 24–25, Reuters/Edgard Garrido, 14–15, Reuters/Stringer/Philippines, 4–5, UPI/Chris Carson, 28–29, ZUMA Press/Bill Gentile, 6–7, ZUMA Press/Library of Congress, 8–9; NOAA, 18–19; Science Source, 20–21; Shutterstock: behindlens, design elements; leonello calvetti, cover, 3, 31; saphireleo, cover; xpixel, design elements

Every effort has been made to contact copyright holders of material reproduced in this book. Any omissions will be rectified in subsequent printings if notice is given to the publisher.

All the internet addresses (URLs) given in this book were valid at the time of going to press. However, due to the dynamic nature of the internet, some addresses may have changed, or sites may have changed or ceased to exist since publication. While the author and publisher regret any inconvenience this may cause readers, no responsibility for any such changes can be accepted by either the author or the publisher.

CONTENTS

AWESOME POWER

HURRICANE CATEGORIES

5

4

3

2

1

A hurricane's strength is based on its wind speed. Hurricanes are ranked on a scale from 1 to 5. Category 5 hurricanes are the most powerful storms in the world.

Huge ocean waves pound the shore. Ferocious winds hammer buildings and uproot trees. A hurricane's power is an awesome sight. Every year, nature's most powerful storms bring destruction around the world. Read on to learn about the worst hurricanes ever seen.

CATEGORY

1	2	3	4	5
119 to 153 kph (74 to 95 mph)	154 to 177 kph (96 to 110 mph)	178 to 209 kph (111 to 130 mph)	210 to 249 kph (131 to 155 mph)	250+ kph (156+ mph)

wind speeds (kilometres/miles per hour)

HURRICANE ANDREW

Location:
Florida, USA, and
The Bahamas

Date:
16–28 August
1992

Rating:

5
4
3
2
1

Hurricane Andrew slammed into Florida, USA, on 24 August 1992. Its winds reached 266 kilometres (165 miles) per hour. The Category 5 storm was incredibly destructive. It toppled trees and crushed whole communities.

FACT

Hurricane Andrew was one of the costliest storms in history. It caused $26.5 billion worth of damage in the United States alone.

DISASTER IN GALVESTON

Location:
Galveston, Texas, USA

Date:
27 August –
8 September 1900

Rating:

5
4
3
2
1

Galveston, Texas, USA, was a booming city in 1900. Then a powerful hurricane hit. The storm created a massive 4.7-metre (15.5-foot) **storm surge**. It pushed a wall of **debris** across the city. Few buildings were left standing.

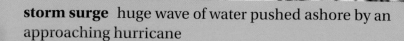

storm surge huge wave of water pushed ashore by an approaching hurricane

The Galveston hurricane was the deadliest natural disaster in US history. The storm killed between 6,000 and 12,000 people.

debris scattered pieces of something that has been broken or destroyed

THE GREAT HURRICANE OF 1780

Location:
Caribbean Sea

Date:
9–20 October 1780

Rating:

5
4
3
2
1

The Great Hurricane of 1780 may have affected the American Revolutionary War (1775–1783). The storm destroyed most of the British ships in the Caribbean Sea. This may have helped America to win its **independence**.

FACT

The Great Hurricane killed more than 20,000 people. It is the deadliest hurricane ever recorded in the Atlantic Ocean.

HISTORY'S DEADLIEST STORM

Location:
Bhola, Bangladesh

Date:
7–13 November 1970

Rating:

5
4
3
2
1

Bhola, Bangladesh, was hit by history's deadliest storm in 1970. The powerful **cyclone** created a 6.1-metre- (20-foot-) high storm surge. It swept away homes, trees, animals and people. Up to 500,000 people died in the disaster.

FACT

Before hitting land, the deadly Bhola storm sank a huge ship weighing more than 4,500 tonnes.

cyclone storm with strong winds that blow around a central point

A RECORD-SETTING STORM

Location:
south-western Mexico

Date:
20–24 October 2015

Rating:

5
4
3
2
1

In October 2015, Hurricane Patricia set a new record. Its winds reached 322 kilometres (200 miles) per hour. After making **landfall** in Mexico, the storm caused severe flooding. It caused about $300 million worth of damage.

landfall area where a hurricane moves over land

FACT

Hurricane Patricia weakened very quickly after hitting land. It dropped from a Category 5 storm to a **remnant low** in less than 24 hours.

remnant low remains of a hurricane with winds less than 63 kilometres (39 miles) per hour

HURRICANE KATRINA

Location:
south-eastern
United States

Date:
23–30 August
2005

Rating:

5
4
3
2
1

Hurricane Katrina was one of the worst disasters in US history. It slammed into the Gulf Coast with winds of 193 kilometres (120 miles) per hour. It brought a storm surge that overwhelmed **levees** in New Orleans, Louisiana. Most of the city was flooded.

FACT

Hurricane Katrina claimed the lives of more than 1,800 people. The storm left more than 1 million people homeless.

levee bank of earth or structure on the side of a river to keep it from overflowing

HURRICANE CAMILLE

Location:
south-east United States, Cuba

Date:
14–22 August 1969

Rating:

5
4
3
2
1

Hurricane Camille roared into the Gulf Coast in August 1969. The storm brought winds close to 322 kilometres (200 miles) per hour. It also dropped up to 79 centimetres (31 inches) of rain. Camille caused close to $1.4 billion worth of destruction across the south-eastern United States.

FACT

Hurricane Camille created a 7.6-metre (25-foot) storm surge that left large ships stranded on beaches.

1935 LABOR DAY HURRICANE

Location:
Florida Keys,
Florida

Date:
August 29–
September 10, 1935

Rating:

The 1935 Labor Day Hurricane devastated the Florida Keys in the United States. The storm's winds reached 298 kilometres (185 miles) per hour. A huge storm surge pushed over a train. A ship was blown more than 4.8 kilometres (3 miles) **inland**.

FACT

The 1935 Labor Day Hurricane claimed the lives of more than 400 people.

HURRICANE DONNA

Location:
Puerto Rico, Cuba,
The Bahamas,
eastern United States

Date:
29 August –
13 September 1960

Rating:

5
4
3
2
1

In 1960, Hurricane Donna raged for more than two weeks. It first hit the Florida Keys, USA. Then it turned north-east to pound North Carolina. The storm next hit Rhode Island with winds of 209 kilometres (130 miles) per hour. It finally **dissipated** over Canada.

FACT

Hurricane Donna travelled more than 3,200 kilometres (2,000 miles).

dissipate break down and disappear

MIGHTY MITCH

Location:
Central America

Date:
22 October –
5 November 1998

Rating:

5
4
3
2
1

Hurricane Mitch hit Central America in 1998. The storm dumped more than 1.8 metres (6 feet) of rain on Honduras and Nicaragua. The water rushed down the mountains. **Mudslides** wiped out entire villages.

mudslide flow of rock, soil and debris mixed with water

SUPERSTORM SANDY

Location:
Jamaica, Cuba, north-east United States

Date:
22–31 October 2012

Rating:

5
4
3
2
1

In 2012, Hurricane Sandy became the second-costliest storm in US history. It washed away beaches. It flooded entire cities. Thousands of homes were destroyed. Sandy caused the deaths of more than 200 people. It caused nearly $75 billion worth of damage.

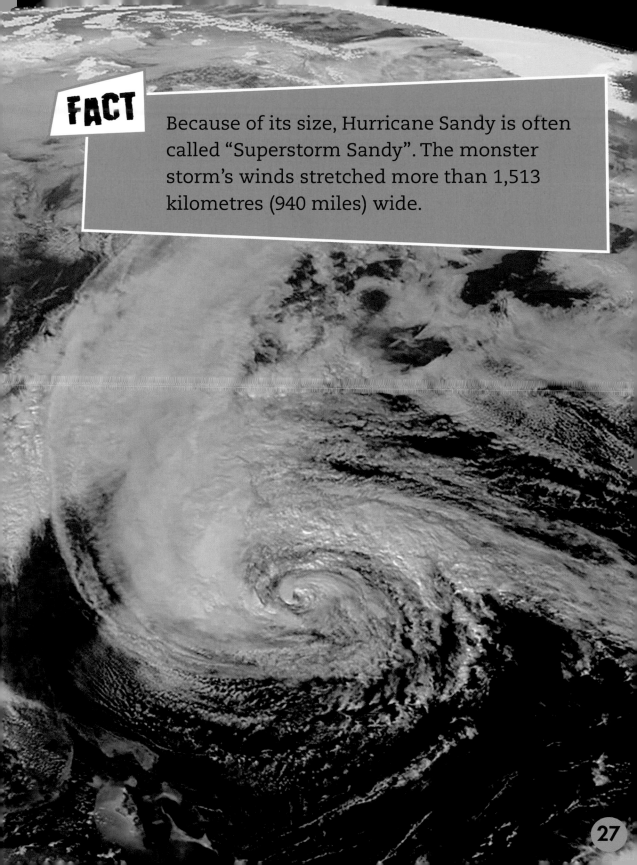

FACT

Because of its size, Hurricane Sandy is often called "Superstorm Sandy". The monster storm's winds stretched more than 1,513 kilometres (940 miles) wide.

SURVIVING HURRICANES

People need to be prepared in places where hurricanes strike. When a hurricane warning is announced, people board up windows. They stock up on food and water. They prepare to **evacuate** if necessary. People must respect a hurricane's power and take steps to stay safe.

DISASTER EMERGENCY KIT

An emergency kit can be very helpful in case of a hurricane. A good kit should include these items:

- ✔ first-aid kit
- ✔ torch
- ✔ battery-powered radio
- ✔ extra batteries
- ✔ blankets

- ✔ bottled water
- ✔ tinned and dried food
- ✔ tin opener
- ✔ whistle to alert rescue workers

evacuate leave a dangerous place and go somewhere safer

GLOSSARY

cyclone storm with strong winds that blow around a central point

debris scattered pieces of something that has been broken or destroyed

dissipate break down and disappear

evacuate leave a dangerous place and go somewhere safer

independence freedom from the control of other people or things

inland away from the sea

landfall area where a hurricane moves over land

levee bank of earth or structure built on the side of a river to keep it from overflowing

mudslide flow of rock, earth and debris mixed with water

remnant low remains of a hurricane with winds less than 63 kilometres (39 miles) per hour

storm surge huge wave of water pushed ashore by an approaching hurricane

READ MORE

Hurricane and Tornado (Eyewitness),
Jack Challoner (DK Children, 2014)

Storms and Hurricanes, Emily Bone
(Usborne Publishing, 2012)

Surviving Hurricanes (Children's True Stories:
Natural Disasters), Elizabeth Raum (Raintree, 2012)

WEBSITES

www.dkfindout.com/uk/earth/weather/hurricanes

Find out more about hurricanes and how they are formed.

**news.bbc.co.uk/cbbcnews/hi/newsid_2290000/
newsid_2296600/2296669.stm**

Discover more about hurricanes, following news stories
from around the world.

COMPREHENSION QUESTIONS

1. Hurricanes are the most powerful and deadliest storms in the world. Which hurricane killed the most people in history? Which one caused the most damage?

2. Explain what you would do during a hurricane warning.

3. Look at the chart on pages 4–5. What are the wind speeds for each category of hurricane?

INDEX